Halloween

Fiction and Nonfiction Paired Reading

SKELETON FOR DINNER
Margery Cuyler

Halloween
Warren Rylands

Halloween

Fiction and Nonfiction Paired Reading

Go to www.openlightbox.com and enter this book's unique code.

BOOK CODE

AVW47269

Explore your **AV2 Fiction** interactive eBook!

Even spooky skeletons, ghosts, and ghouls get scared sometimes! Big Witch and Little Witch have made stew, and now they want to have their friends for dinner. When Skeleton mistakes the guest list for a menu, he takes off running, and Ghost and Ghoul soon join him too!

Skeleton for Dinner
First Published by

Albert Whitman & Co.

2

The Benefits of Paired Fiction and Nonfiction

Pairing fiction and nonfiction titles is a research-based educational approach proven to enhance student outcomes. It improves reading comprehension, increases engagement, expands background knowledge, and helps build vocabulary.

Each paired fiction title is read aloud by professional narrators, offering students the opportunity to listen and learn at their own pace. Every paired nonfiction title comes with a host of digital features designed to engage all learning styles and build a solid foundation for future growth. Both fiction and nonfiction titles are sure to captivate even the most reluctant reader with their dynamic visuals and curated content.

AV2 Fiction Readalong Navigation

1-Year Grades K–5 Premium Fiction Subscription ISBN
979-8-8745-1655-0

The digital components of this book are guaranteed to stay active for at least five years from the date of publication.

One day, Big Witch and Little Witch decided to brew a stew.

They added all their favorite ingredients. Shark fins and snake skins, spider silk and centaur's milk, catfish whiskers and banshee blisters.

Big Witch took a taste. "This is sooooo yummy," she said. "Let's invite our friends for dinner."

"What fun!" said Little Witch. "I'll make a list. Ghost, Ghoul, and..."

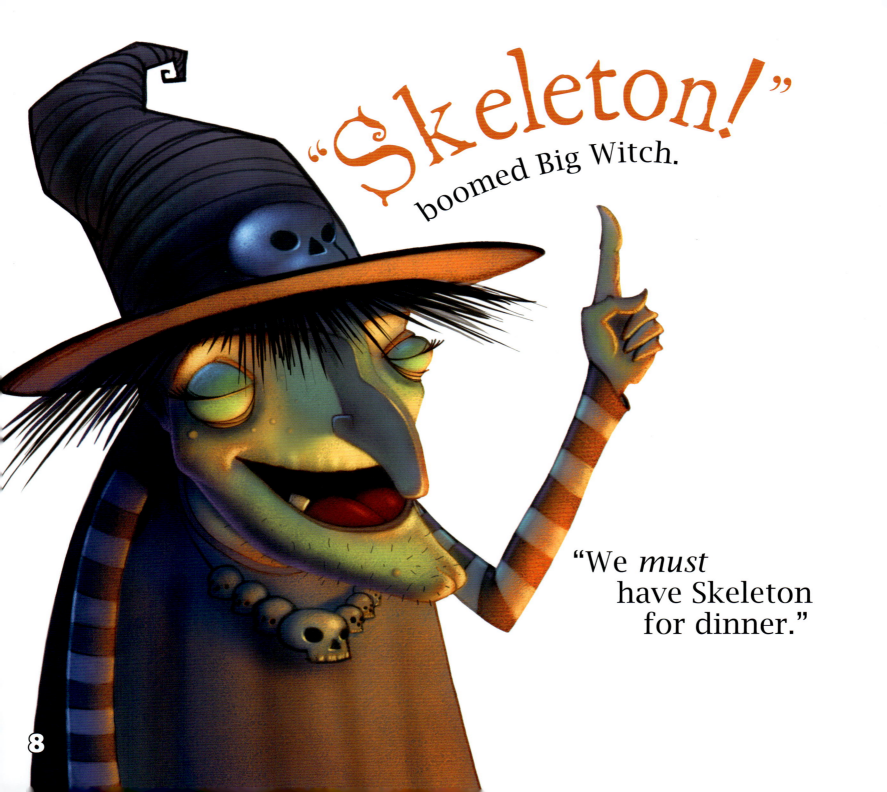

Just then, Skeleton was clickity-clacking up the hill.

As he reached the top, he saw Little Witch's list pegged to a tree. He heard what Big Witch said to Little Witch.

"I think they want to have me for dinner!" cried Skeleton. "I don't want to be eaten!" His bones began to quake and shake.

Before the witches saw him, he rat-a-bat-tatted down the hill...

and jingle-jangled as fast as he could to Ghost's.

"The witches want me in their stew,
and they want to eat you too," he screeched.

"Ohhhhh nooooo!" wailed Ghost, and she floated after Skeleton.

They scooted by the graveyard where Ghoul was shoveling dirt.

"Where are you going in such a hurry?" he asked.

"The witches want us in their stew, and they want to eat you too," said Skeleton.

"Yikes," shouted Ghoul, "let's go hide."
And he dashed after the others.

Back on the hill, Little Witch said, "I'm off to invite our friends for dinner." And away she flew on her broomstick.

But when she got to Skeleton's, he was nowhere to be seen.

"Maybe he's at Ghost's," thought Little Witch.

But she didn't see anyone at Ghost's house either.

"I bet they're all at Ghoul's," thought Little Witch.

She zoomed to the graveyard. It was as quiet as the moon.

"Where is everybody?" said Little Witch. "How can I invite our friends for dinner if they've all disappeared?"

She flew back to the top of the hill. "I couldn't find anybody at home," she told Big Witch. "I guess we'll have to eat our stew all by ourselves. And I was really looking forward to our party."

She took down the sign and began to cry.

Crow flew down and picked it up. "I think I know what's wrong," he cawed and off he flew flapping his wings.

He went to Skeleton's. No Skeleton.

He went to Ghost's. No Ghost.

He went to Ghoul's. No Ghoul.

And then he saw footprints leading into the woods...

He followed them to a big tree.

Up, up, up he flew.

"What are *you* doing here?" asked Skeleton. "I came to tell you that the witches want you to come for dinner."
"You mean they want to *eat* us for dinner," said Skeleton.

"No, they want to have you for dinner," said Crow. "That means *invite* you for dinner."

"Ohhhhh," said Skeleton. "Well, that's different from what I thought. I'm hungry. Let's go!"

So Skeleton, Ghost, and Ghoul came down from the tree.

They picked some poison ivy to take to the witches for their stew.

When they got to the top of the hill, the witches were so happy to see them, their faces lit up like jack-o'-lanterns.

"Come and eat!" shouted Big Witch.

"Have a seat!" shouted Little Witch.

"And we'll give you a treat," said both witches together.

"It looks so yummy," said Skeleton, "that I wish I had a tummy!"

And they all had fun eating the witches' stew together.

32

Halloween

Fiction and Nonfiction Paired Reading

Go to www.openlightbox.com and enter this book's unique code.

BOOK CODE

AVW47269

Explore your **AV2 Nonfiction** interactive eBook!

Did you know that Halloween is known for its ghosts, witches, and scary stories? Bats, black cats, and brightly lit pumpkins called jack-o'-lanterns are all symbols of the holiday. Discover these and other interesting facts in *Halloween*.

Halloween
First Published by

34

Watch
Video content brings each page to life.

Browse
Thumbnails make navigation simple.

Listen
Hear each page read aloud.

Read
Follow along with text on the screen.

AV2 Nonfiction Readalong Navigation

Audio
Listen to the entire book read aloud.

Video
High resolution videos turn each spread into an optic readalong.

OPTIMIZED FOR

☑ **TABLETS**

☑ **SMART BOARDS**

☑ **COMPUTERS**

☑ **AND MUCH MORE!**

1-Year Grades K–5 Premium Fiction Subscription ISBN
979-8-8745-1655-0

The digital components of this book are guaranteed to stay active for at least five years from the date of publication.

Halloween

In this book, you will learn about

- what it is
- when it is celebrated
- how it is celebrated

and much more!

Halloween began as an ancient harvest festival called *Samhain*, or "end of summer."

Today, Halloween is celebrated on October 31. It is very popular in the United States and Canada.

Halloween is known for its ghosts, witches, and scary stories.

People may decorate their homes and gardens to look like haunted houses.

43

Pumpkin carvings and costume parties are also a large part of Halloween.

Children dress in costumes on Halloween. They go trick-or-treating for candy.

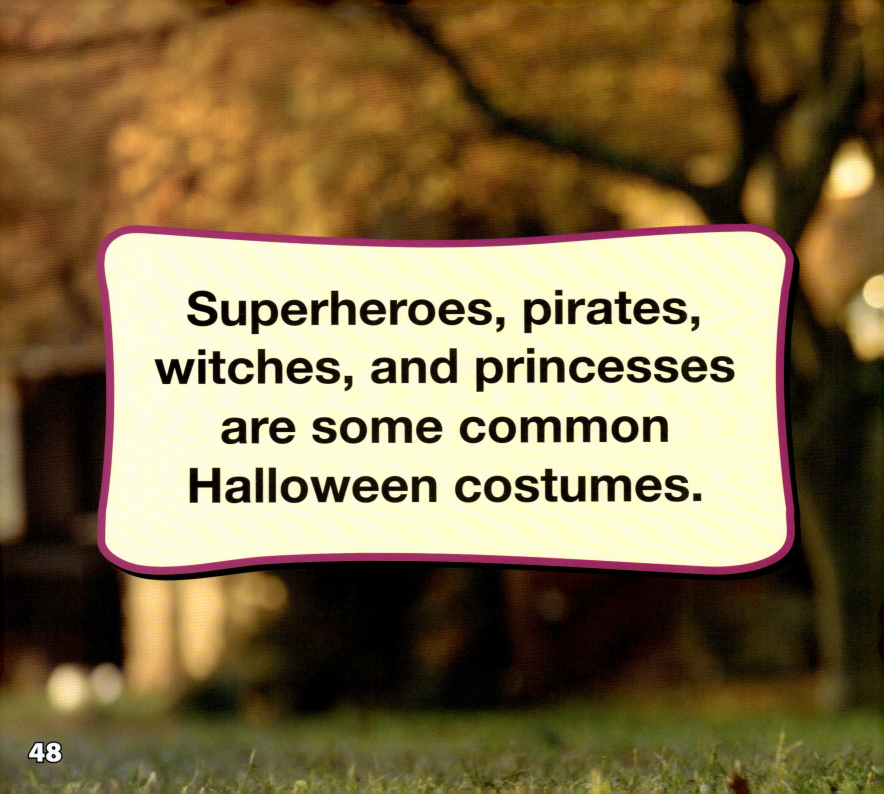

Superheroes, pirates, witches, and princesses are some common Halloween costumes.

Black and orange are the traditional colors of Halloween.

Bats, black cats, and brightly lit pumpkins called jack-o'-lanterns are all symbols of the holiday.

HALLOWEEN BY THE NUMBERS

"The Legend of Sleepy Hollow" is a ghost story often told on Halloween. It was published in **1820**.

The best-selling Halloween costumes for **2023** included Barbie, princess, and Spider-Man outfits.

About **70 percent** of Americans take part in Halloween **celebrations**.

People in the United States spend more than **$4 billion** on Halloween **costumes** each year.

Samhain was celebrated by the **Celtic** peoples in Europe about **2,500 years ago**.

The world's **largest Halloween parade** is held in New York City.

SIGHT WORDS

Research has shown that as much as 65 percent of all written material published in English is made up of 300 words. These 300 words cannot be taught using pictures or learned by sounding them out. They must be recognized by sight. This book contains 34 common sight words to help young readers improve their reading fluency and comprehension. This book also teaches young readers several important content words, such as proper nouns. These words are paired with pictures to aid in learning and improve understanding.

Page	Sight Words First Appearance
36	an, as, began, end, of, or
39	and, in, is, it, on, states, the, very
41	for, its
43	homes, houses, like, look, may, people, their, to
45	a, also, are, large, part
46	children, go, they
48	some
52	all

Page	Content Words First Appearance
36	Halloween, harvest festival, Samhain, summer
39	Canada, October, United States
41	ghosts, stories, witches
43	gardens
45	carvings, parties
46	candy, costumes, trick-or-treating
48	pirates, princesses, superheroes
50	colors
52	bats, cats, holiday, jack-o'-lanterns, pumpkins, symbols

Published by Lightbox Learning Inc.
276 5th Avenue, Suite 704 #917
New York, NY 10001
Website: www.openlightbox.com

Skeleton for Dinner
First Published by

Halloween
First Published by

Skeleton for Dinner
Written by Margery Cuyler, illustrated by Will Terry.
Text copyright ©2013 by Margery Cuyler
Illustrations copyright ©2013 by Will Terry
Published by arrangement with Albert Whitman & Company

Skeleton for Dinner first published in the United States of America in 2013 by Albert Whitman & Company, 250 South Northwest Highway, Suite 320, Park Ridge, Illinois 60068 USA
ALL RIGHTS RESERVED

Lightbox Learning acknowledges Dreamstime, Getty Images, and Shutterstock as the primary image suppliers for the EyeDiscover *Halloween* title.

Copyright ©2026 Lightbox Learning Inc.
All rights reserved. No part of this publication may be reproduced, stored in a retrieval system, or transmitted in any form or by any means, electronic, mechanical, photocopying, recording, or otherwise, without the prior written permission of the publisher.

Library of Congress Control Number: 2024948025

ISBN 979-8-8745-1920-9 (hardcover)
ISBN 979-8-8745-1921-6 (softcover)
ISBN 979-8-8745-1922-3 (multi-user static eBook)
ISBN 979-8-8745-1924-7 (multi-user interactive eBook)

Printed in Guangzhou, China
1 2 3 4 5 6 7 8 9 0 28 27 26 25 24

112024
102724

Project Coordinator: Priyanka Das
Art Director: Terry Paulhus
Layout: Jean Faye Rodriguez

These titles are part of our Premium Fiction digital subscription

1-Year Grades K–5 Premium Fiction Subscription ISBN
979-8-8745-1655-0

Access dozens of Paired Reading and Storytime titles with our Premium Fiction digital subscription.
Sign up for a FREE trial at www.openlightbox.com/trial